MINISTRY OF PUBLIC BUILDING AND WORKS

A look round the MONASTERIES of North-East Yorkshire

by **ALAN PHILLIPS, M.A., OXON.**

LONDON
HER MAJESTY'S STATIONERY OFFICE
1962

First published 1962
Fourth impression 1970

The drawings which head
the texts describing each
monastery are
by William Richardson.
They appeared in *Monastic Ruins of Yorkshire*,
by Rev. Edward Churton, 1843

Rievaulx Abbey

MONKS we think of as men of tranquil mind, attained by days of repetition and repose. At the opposite pole of the Middle Ages, knights suggest the questing spirit, fired by a life of colour and movement. Which did more to civilize Europe: monasticism or chivalry? Their influence has scarcely a point of comparison, yet both were vital. To understand our past we have to read about monasteries and view their remains with the same eagerness that we give to castles. North-east Yorkshire is one of the regions where they cluster in plenty to enlighten us.

Monasteries include abbeys and priories, the distinction being one of status; usually a priory was smaller, perhaps having started as an offshoot from or dependency on an abbey. At either type of establishment the number of buildings and the way they were grouped will be found not to vary much. Dominating all was the church, focus of the monk's waking hours, with its main divisions from west to east into nave, transepts, quire, and presbytery. Next to it lay the cloister, round which stood the biggest or most important blocks of buildings. Those contained the refectory, or frater—the hall for meals—with the kitchen beside it; the chapter house, assembly point for communal affairs; the dormitory, or dorter, and the latrines, or reredorter. There were almost invariably in one or other of those ranges a parlour, warming house, and almonry, and there might be a library. Other necessary parts of the foundation, remoter from the church, were the infirmary and guest house. The precinct was surrounded by a wall and entered through a gatehouse. Frequently barns and fishponds lay beyond.

Few things spring to life so quickly as tumbled stone and mounds; and we easily picture those groups of devoted people going about their regular prayer and toil. Their normal day was punctuated by services at what were known as canonical hours, starting just after midnight and going on until early evening: matins, lauds, prime, terce, sext, none, vespers, compline. High Mass and assembly in chapter had also to be fitted in. Administration was minutely organized, so we can allot the duties of numerous officials. The precentor was responsible for singing and processions, and might serve as librarian and archivist; the department of the sacrist covered vestments, plate, ornaments, and bells; the cellarer, whom Cardinal Gasquet dubbed 'the Martha of the establishment', dealt with fairs and markets, ordered wholesale provisions; clothes and bedding were the concern of the chamberlain; the almoner gave doles to the poor; while refectorer and kitchener, infirmarer and guest master, governed each a clear province.

Some divergences between the monastic Orders must be touched on. Benedictines followed the classic regulations laid down by St. Benedict at Monte Cassino in 529, and were the agency that brought the Roman type of Christianity to England. St. Augustine was one of them. Augustinian communities arose among priests at non-monastic churches, developing into an Order wherein all members of convents were priests. There were also Augustinian nunneries. Cistercians, named from Cîteaux in Burgundy, sought austere ways of living and so chose sites far from towns; they forbade silk, used precious metals only for the chalice, had crosses of painted wood and censers of copper. Emphasizing labour rather than study, they grew crops and kept sheep, with help from lay brothers. Stricter still were Carthusians, from Chartreuse in Dauphiné, who aspired to journey to salvation alone. Of the houses visited in this book, Whitby was a Benedictine abbey; Kirkham and Gisborough were Augustinian priories; Rievaulx and Byland, Cistercian abbeys; Mount Grace was a Carthusian priory of charterhouse.

It happens that at each of the six monasteries a different feature is in the best state of preservation. At Kirkham the gatehouse; at Byland the west front; at Rievaulx the presbytery; at Mount Grace the cloister; at Gisborough the east end; at Whitby the north transept: these are among the heirlooms handed down from the Plantagenets for travellers today to inspect. They are strung out in that order in the following pages, presented as to a motorist on a zigzag course from York. This book is designed to be only an illustrated souvenir; the visitor in search of fuller information is advised to consult *Abbeys*, an official publication by the Ministry of Public Building and Works, which looks after these six monasteries among many others.

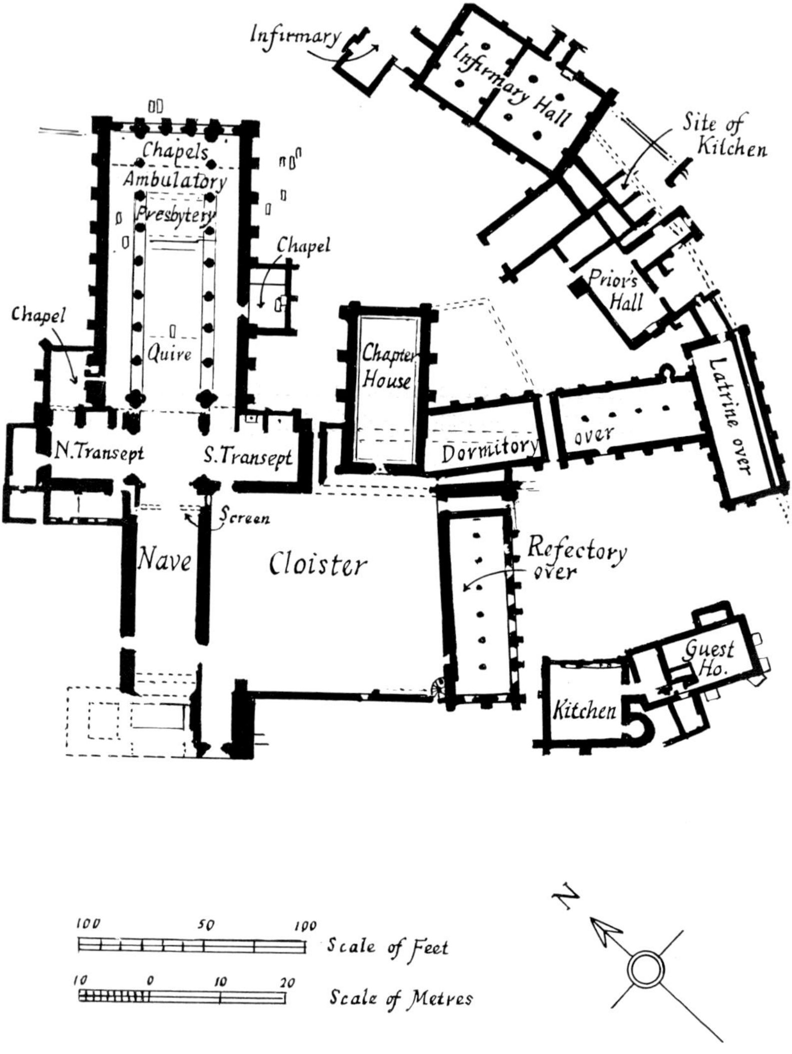

Infirmary
Infirmary Hall
Site of Kitchen
Chapels
Ambulatory
Presbytery
Chapel
Chapel
Quire
Prior's Hall
Chapter House
Latrine over
N.Transept
S.Transept
Dormitory
over
Screen
Nave
Cloister
Refectory over
Guest Ho.
Kitchen
100
50
100
Scale of Feet
10
0
10
20
Scale of Metres
N

Kirkham Priory

Being on the left bank of a boundary stream, Kirkham, alone among the houses to be described, lies in the East Riding; many would say in the most delectable spot in that riding, where the Derwent clatters under a stone bridge and over a weir, passing a hamlet clad with creepers and copper beeches.

Of the buildings, cared for since 1927 by the Ministry of Public Building and Works, only a few fragments stand to murmur of past glory; but the ground plan will be clear to the most casual observer if he makes for the eminence at the south-east corner of the grassy enclosure. There he will take in with one glimpse the gatehouse; a piece of the east end of the church; south and west walls of the cloister; masonry between the dormitory and latrine blocks; and the crescent of the main drain whose course accounts

The 13th-century gatehouse is enriched with heraldic carving and figures of saints and legendary heroes

for the siting of many structures. In that single view all essential details of Kirkham can be comprehended.

A legend is attached to its foundation. The lord of Helmsley, Walter L'Espec, a big man with black hair, great beard, and a voice like a trumpet, lost his only son who fell from a horse near this place. We read of the historical Walter that he had no surviving children to carry on his name: but not that he never had a son. In memory of the youth, so the tale goes, he established this priory for Augustinian canons in 1122 or soon after. We shall meet Walter again at Rievaulx, where he was to found an abbey for Cistercians. At one of these houses he is supposed to have made retreat, died, and been buried. His uncle William, who had encouraged him to endow Kirkham, was brought from his rectory to be its first prior.

The two monasteries were in close communion, and although Kirkham in the end remained Augustinian, it must have looked about 1140 as if they would merge. Waltheof, prior of Kirkham, already had gone over to the

Before taking meals in the refectory, canons washed their hands here. The Latin term is lavatorium

Cistercians. There exists a document setting forth an agreement which seems to imply that the canons he had left would surrender the priory with all fixed property to Rievaulx, and in return would be admitted, as many as so desired, into the Cistercian Order; while the succeeding prior of Kirkham and others who intended to stay aloof would take with them all movable items disliked by that Order, costly chalices and crosses, sumptuous vestments, and stained glass, to new monastic premises at Linton-on-Ouse. But what befell we do not know.

Anyway in the thirteenth century a large-scale rebuilding of this church was begun from the east. The new presbytery and quire became the favourite burial ground of lords of Helmsley of the de Ros family between 1258 and 1343. Like most similar houses, Kirkham was then heavily in debt; one cause was the sale of corrodies, or life pensions, to benefactors who ended their days in the precincts. In its later years there were fewer than twenty canons, and the annual revenue came to £269. John Kelwik

This Romanesque arch of three orders formed the entrance to the refectory from the south side of the cloister

was holding office as prior when Henry the Eighth's Commissioners of the North arrived in Yorkshire to carry out the Act suppressing the smaller religious houses. The end here came on 8th December 1538 and was, for those times, undramatic: 'we have quyetlye takine the surrenders and dissolved the monasteries' of Kirkham and many others, reported the Commissioners to Thomas Cromwell.

The consecrated but no longer secluded ground is still entered through the ruins of a magnificent gatehouse, whose north front is an attractive composition of the late thirteenth century. A graceful shape is embellished with carving, statuary, and heraldry. The arch is enclosed in a gable and elaborately moulded; windows have geometric tracery and panelled sills; a row of five leafy gables pricks up into a panelled parapet; and the façade is bounded by buttresses carried up as pinnacles. There are figures of Our

Lord and SS. Philip and Bartholomew; groups depicting David and Goliath, St. George and the Dragon; shields with the arms of England and of seven baronial families.

Another architectural gem is the place where the canons before entering the refectory washed their hands in leaded troughs, since removed. This will be noticed in the wall of the west alley of the cloister, next to a winding stair. Of the same period as the gatehouse, it has geometric stone patterns in two bays that rise on slender shafts to moulded arches.

Presbytery and quire of the new church had eight bays and extended 125 feet; north and south aisles were added, though the nave continued to have none. We can see that the middle east window was a triplet and that of each aisle a single lancet. In the easternmost and narrowest bay was a platform with three or five altars. The plan of the monastic buildings abounds in abnormalities; for instance, the refectory, over its vaulted basement, is set obliquely, not at right angles, to other principal features. It must have been a splendid room some 85 feet long. The cloister, where now a cherry tree flourishes, was 96 feet east to west by 114 feet north to south. Treatment of doorways leading to and from it will repay attention.

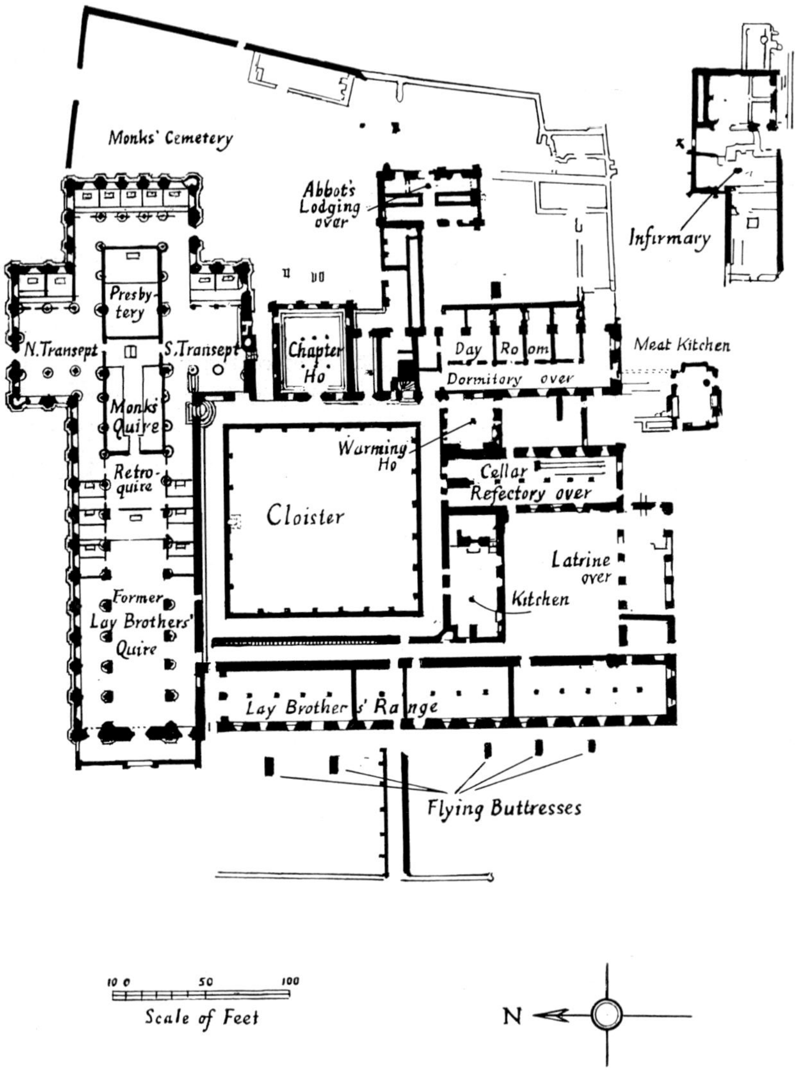

Monks' Cemetery
Abbot's Lodging over
Infirmary
Presbytery
N. Transept
S. Transept
Chapter Ho
Day Room
Dormitory over
Meat Kitchen
Monks' Quire
Warming Ho
Cellar
Refectory over
Retro-quire
Cloister
Latrine over
Kitchen
Former Lay Brothers' Quire
Lay Brothers' Range
Flying Buttresses
10 0 50 100
Scale of Feet
N

Byland Abbey

The southern slopes of the Hambleton Hills are hospitable today, with springs at the feet of hanging woods of oak and ash; but eight centuries ago they were a swamp. Before the Cistercian colony arrived there from Stocking to occupy the present site of Byland Abbey at All Saints' tide in 1177, years must have been spent in draining the ground and putting up temporary buildings.

Their third abbot, Philip, recorded their journeying and pioneering under his predecessor Roger, who ruled for the astonishing period of 54 years (1142-96). They began as a branch of Furness Abbey in Lancashire. After early adventures, they were given by Roger de Mowbray in 1143 a refuge at Old Byland on the right bank of the Rye. But that was too close to Rievaulx; each monastery could hear the other's bells at all hours,

West front of church seen from remains of gatehouse

'which was not fitting and could by no means be endured'. So the newcomers travelled again, westward over the moor, to Stocking in 1147. Thirty years later came the final move.

Byland Abbey, keeping the old name in the new abode, had a mainly peaceful life. Exemptions and privileges came the way of the monks, who among other Anglo-Saxon customs had a court of *infangentheof* and were free of *grithbreth:* that is, they could arrest and try a thief, or award punishment for breach of the peace. Their benefactor, Roger de Mowbray, was long believed to have been buried here; some bones in a stone coffin removed in 1818 were alleged to be his. The soldier-bishop Wigmund of the Isles closed here in sightless meditation his turbulent career. In September 1322 an invading force of Scots nearly seized Edward the Second after a battle at Shaws Moor; it remains in doubt whether the King was dining at Byland or at Rievaulx, but the Scots pillaged both. When the deed of suppression was signed on the last day of November 1538, Byland had twenty-five monks beside Abbot John Ledes, and an annual income of £295. The land was granted to Sir William Pickering, and passed successfully to the families of Wotton, Stapylton, and Wombwell.

These ruins cannot impress by size like those at Rievaulx or Fountains. The arcading of the presbytery has disappeared, and what has endured of the outward walls is comparatively plain and low. Still standing are parts of the ambulatory, chancel aisles, transepts, nave aisles, and west front, to consider only the church from east to west. One of the most appealing views is gained from the relic of the gatehouse, a semicircular arch that spans the lane to Oldstead.

Yet this Early English church when completed soon after 1200 was the biggest carried out as a unified task by Cistercians in England, and was ranked by Lord Grimthorpe twenty-sixth in size among our churches. It was 330 feet long and 140 feet wide across the transepts. It contained a rarity in a continuous aisle west of the transepts as well as east; another aisle or ambulatory ran east of the quire as well as north and south. There were twelve bays to the nave: five formed the monks' quire, and seven to the west were for use of the lay brothers recruited by this Order. No Lady

Traces of painting may be discerned on the ruined wall. The tiles in the foreground are green and yellow

Chapel was needed since all Cistercian churches were dedicated to the Virgin Mary. For sheer size the cloister was remarkable, its square of 145 feet exceeding those at Rievaulx and Fountains.

If the other elevations were austere, according to the conventions, every visitor recalls how ornamental is the detail on the west front. There are three doorways copiously moulded, the arch in the centre being a trefoil, that on the north pointed, that on the south semicircular. A line of corbels, now much decayed, supported the roof of the vanished porch. Next above come three lancets in a row of blind arcading, and from this storey a buttress thrusts an octagonal turret like a delicate finger skyward. A huge wheel window 26 feet across must have been a lovely creation.

Stones recovered in the course of excavation, particularly the capitals of the great piers, show carving of artistic excellence and wide variety of subject. 'A distinctive loop at the base of the foliage is so persistent that it might fairly be called a Byland detail,' states Sir Charles Peers. It may be spotted that capitals on shafts of the central entrance are plain to the south and sculptured to the north. This is the only Cistercian church in England wherein piers and arches of the ground storey were carried round the whole edifice; also probably the earliest to use the pointed arch decoratively as well as structurally. Typical fragments of its adornment are stored in the museum assembled by the Ministry of Public Building and Works, which has looked after the monument since 1921.

Almost the entire church was paved with green and yellow glazed tiles in geometric designs. Two chapels in the south transept, where the floors are nearly perfect, give some sketch of the scintillating effect. The interior was whitewashed and its walls were lined with a masonry pattern in red, the capitals being picked out in red also. There were wall paintings in the nave.

Most interesting of the other remains are the chapter house, square-ended and vaulted, with two ranges of seats round its walls; the parlour, where the monks were allowed to converse (and nowhere else); the refectory, about 100 feet long by 31 feet wide, at right angles to the cloister as usual with this Order, and next to it the warming house which contained the only fire apart from kitchen and infirmary; the narrow western range, a double storey of eighteen bays and 275 feet long that housed the lay brothers and was the oldest part of the monastery erected in permanent form; and the strangely shaped infirmary, with reddened tiles hinting at the existence of a hearth.

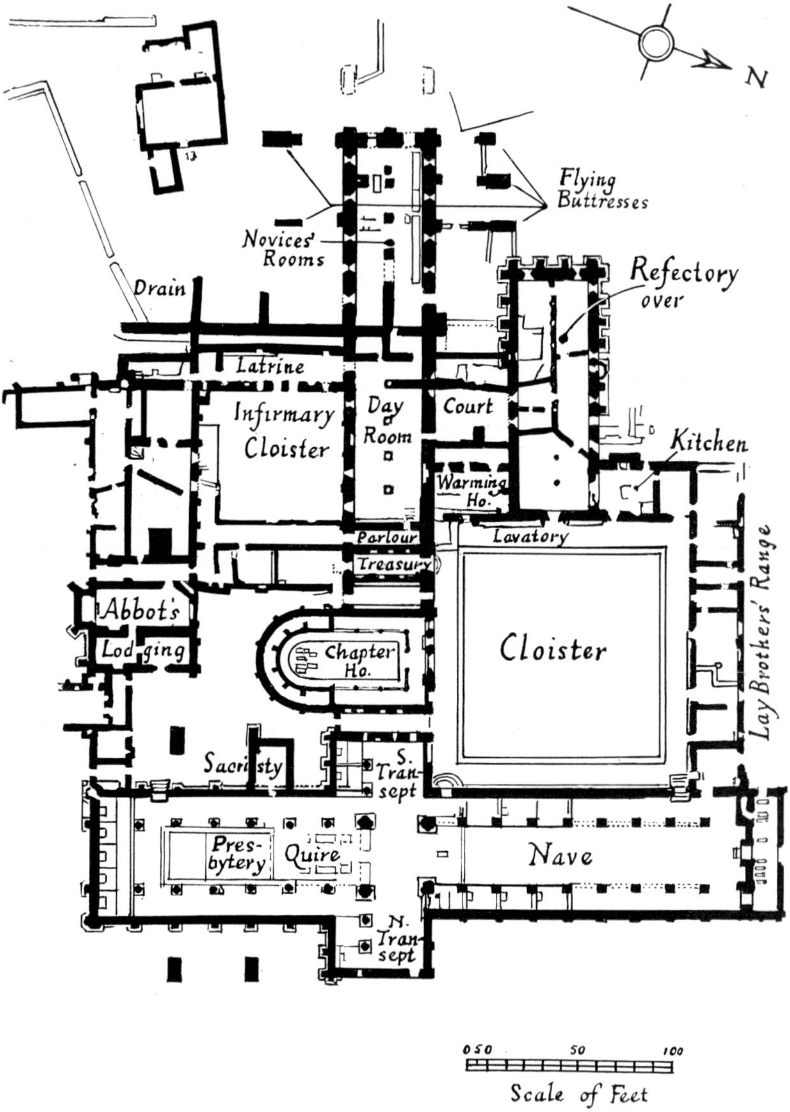

N
Flying Buttresses
Novices' Rooms
Refectory over
Drain
Latrine
Infirmary Cloister
Day Room
Court
Kitchen
Warming Ho.
Lavatory
Parlour
Treasury
Lay Brothers' Range
Abbot's Lodging
Chapter Ho.
Cloister
Sacristy
S. Transept
Presbytery
Quire
Nave
N. Transept
0 50 50 100
Scale of Feet

Rievaulx Abbey

When the talk turns on unforgettable views, someone is sure to propose the first sight of Rievaulx Abbey if he has done homage to it by the classic approach past the terrace Thomas Duncombe laid out in 1758. From this plateau contrived jointly by nature and man, with its flanking temples, and its evergreen plantations as shields to east and north, one looks over Ryedale where it is joined by four lesser dales and is clothed with cornfield and pasture, heath and limestone crag. The prospect is glorious but the valley narrow; the ground below the ruins falls so sharply westward that the builders had to disregard an elementary rule, setting the church nearly south-north instead of east-west. But in describing its features, practice has always been, and will be here, to write as if they followed the customary orientation.

The chapter house (foreground) and monastic buildings

In early monastic times the river Rye divided here the lands of black-haired Walter L'Espec, whom we met at Kirkham, and Roger de Mowbray, noted at Byland. It flowed much farther east than nowadays. Walter bestowed on William, first abbot of Rievaulx, and his dozen monks nine carucates of land—a carucate was as much as could be tilled by one plough in a year—but they possessed only the eastern slopes of the dale when Byland was set up on the other side. By grants from the Crown, the see of Durham, and eventually Roger himself, Rievaulx was permitted to cut dykes to annex grassland, and by at least three separate enterprises deflected the parent stream, which from about 1203 was channelled on the west of the dale as it is today.

The ruins are extensive and majestic enough to give a vivid idea of how men lived who converted this 'place of horror and waste solitude', as seen by one monkish chronicler, to the mingled ruggedness and grace that

North aisle with south transept beyond

made Dorothy Wordsworth lyrical and sent Cotman, Girtin, and Turner to their sketch-books.

Rievaulx was the earliest Cistercian abbey in the north. Its foundation in 1131 was due to a mission sent from Clairvaux by St. Bernard only three years after the Order reached England at Waverley in Surrey. Almost at once it began throwing out colonies, Melrose and Warden the first.

From another of those daughter houses, Revesby, Abbot Ailred, 'the Bernard of the North', returned in 1147 to preside for twenty years over Rievaulx. Ascetic and administrator, writer and instructor, diplomat and traveller, St. Ailred is the most substantial and illustrious figure to have belonged to any monastery in this book. During his regime there are said

Seven bays and three tiers of arcading form an outstanding quire and presbytery in Early English style

The tower arch soars 75 feet above the quire floor

All that is left of the refectory

to have been 140 monks and at least 500 lay brothers, 'so that the church swarmed with them, like a hive with bees'.

Then also practically all the monastic buildings as well as the church were raised in permanent form. Nave and parts of transepts go back perhaps to 1135; the range east of the cloister was put up next; side walls of the chapter house are older than the rest; 1170 is probably accurate for the western range and infirmary. About 1200 the refectory with kitchen and warming house superseded earlier work; and around 1230, perhaps in emulation of Whitby or Byland, a fortune was spent on enlarging the eastern half of the church—presbytery, tower, and transepts.

Not surprisingly, the abbey fell into debt; and though it never lost esteem—in 1464 its abbot ranked fourth among dignitaries when the Archbishop of York was installed—its importance slid away. Parts of the chapter house, warming house, and dormitory were taken down, too big for requirements. When the dissolution order was signed on 3rd December 1538 there were twenty-two monks with Abbot Richard Blyton, and the

A reconstruction by Alan Sorrell of what the refectory might have looked like at meal times 800 years ago

income of the house was £351, from which £200 was held to be owing. The site was given to the Earl of Rutland, subsequently passing with the Helmsley estates to the families of Manners, Villiers, and Duncombe. In 1918 the abbey was put under guardianship of the Commissioners of Works (now Ministry of Public Building and Works); and some disused lead was sent to repair the famous Five Sisters window in York Minster.

The outstanding splendour of Rievaulx is found in the eastern half of the church. A paradox has arisen since we are drawn to a Cistercian monastery by glories and graces of Early English architecture that seem to defy the taste of an Order devoted to plainness and simplicity. Yet there it stands, this presbytery and quire of seven bays, with complete system of stone-ribbed vaults, three tiers of arcading to north and south, and double tier of three lancets at the east end. Piers have five shafts to each face; capitals are exquisitely moulded; arches, both circular and pointed, nobly proportioned. Below the triforium—the second storey of arcading—corbels carved with foliage prop fragments of the roof. The stage above is

Abbot William's shrine in the chapter house

the clerestory, with coupled lancets. Flying buttresses are prominent. Everything carries the eye to a point 75 feet aloft where the tower arch opens superbly into the quire.

Detection of the joins in phases of construction is easy. Apart from superior masonry, the newer sandstone is whiter and more finely grained if less warm-hued than the older. The transepts show occasional patchwork of this light and dark. In the north transept one chapel has a notable vaulted roof; it south counterpart is the place to find vestiges of green and yellow glazed tiling that once floored the entire church.

Only in the nave—earliest of large Cistercian naves in Britain and older than any extant in France—did the stern orthodoxy of the Order at that period prevail. There were nine bays, north and south aisles, square piers from which sprang pointed arches. Outside the west front was a lean-to covering the width of the church with a dwarf wall supporting an open arcade. This was known as a Galilee porch, the notion being that the celebrant entering church this way at the head of a procession symbolized Christ going before the disciples into Galilee.

What the cloister was like may be imagined from the reconstruction of five of its round-headed arches on twin shafts standing on a dwarf wall. This cloister was 140 feet square. On the east it gave access to the chapter house, a place with exceptional features: an oblong room with an eastern apse and a western vestibule continued as an aisle right round the apsidal chamber. This was the burial place of abbots, and several tombs remain, but the shrine erected to the first of them, William, a century after his death is an object unparalleled in English chapter houses.

The monks' dormitory on the upper floor of this eastern range ran 320 feet southward from the transept. The refectory, south of the cloister, was a grand room 124 feet by 38 feet, built over a lofty vault entered by a stairway below the pulpit used by the reader at meals. Nearly the same measurements apply to the hall of the infirmary, which appears to have become late the abbot's residence. The western range was allotted, as was normal in this Order, to the lay brothers; it was at first unusually small and inadequate, but at last too spacious, with its upper floor in use as a granary because the brethren had mostly departed.

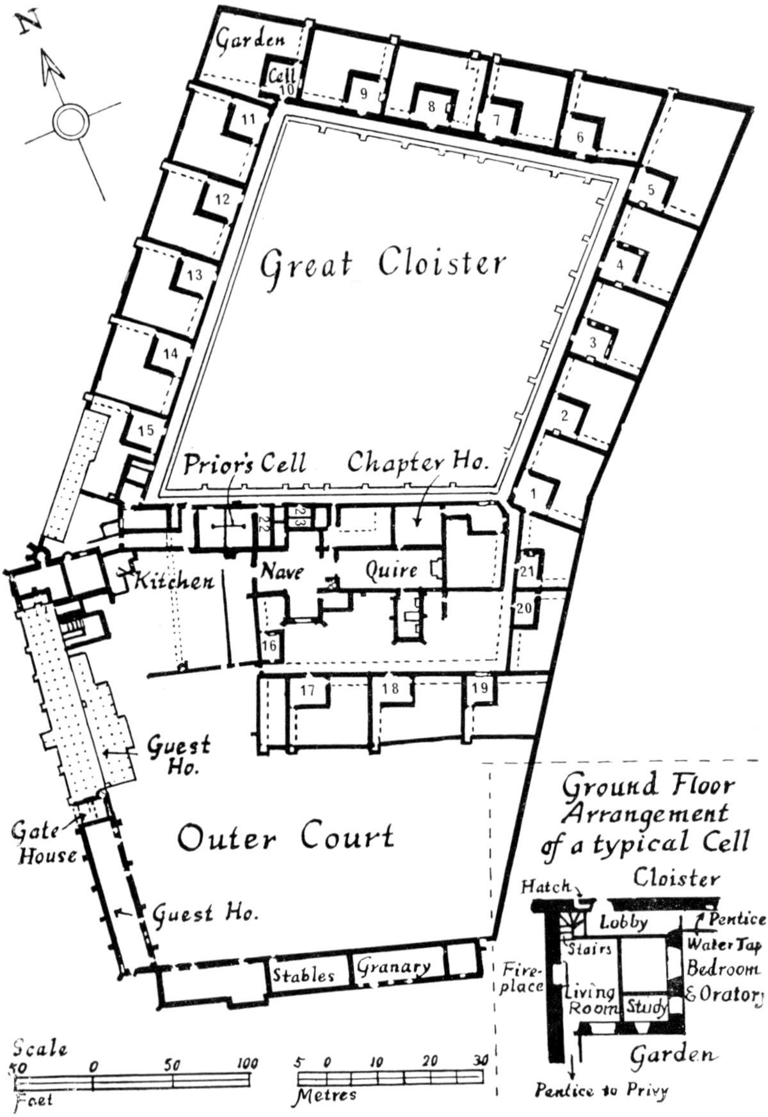

N
Garden
Cell
10
9
8
7
6
5
4
3
2
1
11
12
13
14
15
Great Cloister
Prior's Cell
Chapter Ho.
22
23
Kitchen
Nave
Quire
21
20
16
17
18
19
Guest Ho.
Gate House
Outer Court
Guest Ho.
Stables
Granary
Ground Floor Arrangement of a typical Cell
Cloister
Hatch
Lobby
Pentice
Stairs
Water Tap
Fire-place
Bedroom & Oratory
Living Room
Study
Garden
Pentice to Privy
Scale
50
0
50
100
Feet
5
0
10
20
30
Metres

Mount Grace Priory

Only nine charterhouses were founded in England, and much the most widely and exactly preserved of them is the House of the Assumption of the Most Blessed Virgin and St. Nicholas of Mount Grace in Ingleby. It is therefore the stone equivalent of a set book for anyone studying the Carthusian Order. Since 1953 it has belonged to the National Trust, which placed the ruins in guardianship of the Ministry of Public Building and Works.

It stands at the edge of the Cleveland Hills, protected from east winds by a steep bank planted with oakwoods that used to be more prolific than they are now. The ground can be bright with daffodils and buttercups, but the buildings must always have lacked grandeur, devised as they were to be bare and sombre.

Each monk lived in his own cell and tended a garden behind it. This is what his dwelling was like

The founder was the Duke of Surrey, grandson of the mother of Richard the Second, who licensed the priory in 1398. Construction was not finished when Surrey, deprived of his dukedom after Richard lost the throne, rebelled against the new King and was executed. His remains were reinterred in 1412 at Mount Grace. Ceaseless lawsuits over leases and revenues troubled the monks until about 1445 Henry the Sixth confirmed a charter favourable to them. But Prior Love found time to render St. Bonaventure into English and earned approbation from the Archbishop of Canterbury for writings against the Lollards. Prosperity came so that by 1535 the annual income was £323, placing this among greater monasteries that escaped the first Act of Dissolution. Less fortunate when the next Act raised the level for survival, it was yielded to the King by Prior John Wilson on receipt of a pension towards Christmas 1539. The site was granted to Sir James Strangways; passed to the Lascelles family in 1653; and around 1900 was excavated during the ownership of the ironmaster Sir Lowthian Bell.

Carthusians were more like hermits than other medieval monks. They sought to dwell apart not only from the world but even from one another. Recital of the Divine Office was only partly a communal rite in church; meals in the refectory were only for Sundays and festivals. On ordinary days the monk virtually stayed in his own cell. He would go once or twice to service in church, and perhaps to stroll and chat beside the fishpond, boundary of the world outside. The Carthusian plan thus called for a big cloister set with individual cells and gardens; a modest church, small refectory, and no dormitory.

The precinct is entered through a gatehouse near the middle of a range that forms the short west side of an irregular five-sided area. This range, which had sheltered guests of the priory, was largely turned into a dwelling by Thomas Lascelles in 1654, as initials and date over the porch explain. With battlements and gables, mullioned windows and pantiled roof, it has the quiet dignity of a Stuart manor house, though a gay note is piped by two bronze boys in the front garden. The house is in private occupation.

Carthusian churches were much smaller than their cloisters because this Order had little ceremony

Looking from south-west towards the church tower, which is Perpendicular in style (early 15th century)

Most visitors will be curious about the great cloister. This had diagonals of 379 and 296 feet; its north-west side measures 272 feet while all the others are 231 feet; no sides are parallel and no angles equal. It was surrounded on three sides by double-storey cells and gardens with a continuous pentice or enclosing wall before them and some 50 feet inside the precinct wall. Each cell stood in an angle of its garden and was 27 feet square; it had a stout doorway to the cloister and its ground floor was partitioned into living room, study, oratory, and bedroom, the upper storey probably being a workshop. 'A seclusion within seclusion, of which the double walls were themselves an emblem.' Because the service hatch made a right-angled bend through masonry beside the door, the supplier of food and the inmate could never see each other. Water was piped to each cell.

To refer to the diagram, Cell 8, which exceptionally is not in an angle of its garden, has been reconstructed (apart from the roof) and its exterior gives a good idea of the original appearance. Traces of internal arrangements and windows are seen in Cell 3; of the privy in Cell 7; of recesses for water taps in Cells 11 to 15. The doorway to Cell 1 bears the arms of Archbishop Scrope; the arms on Cells 4 and 5 are those of Gascoigne. Similar small chambers for monks may be examined in the lesser cloister.

In the church, presbytery and quire are ruined save for their north wall. There were never any aisles, as no processions were held. On each side of the nave was added about 1420 a chapel similar to a transept, each with an altar. Masons' marks or other inscriptions may be detected here. The slender tower on four high narrow arches belongs to the same Perpendicular period and is almost intact. Some quire stalls have been excavated.

In continental fashion, the chapter house is placed against the church with no sacristy intervening. An interesting contrast with Cistercian practice is that the place where the monks washed does not here adjoin the refectory but is near the middle of the south cloister wall. It has a projecting basin moulded on the front in a recess with a four-centred head.

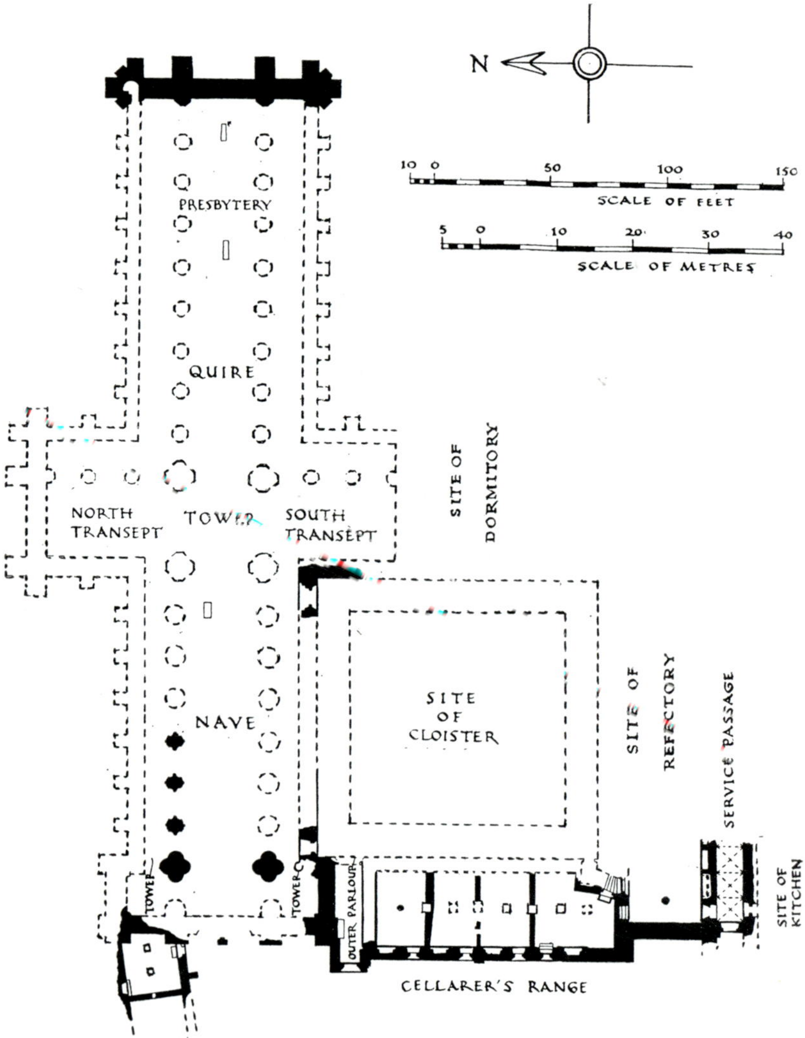
N
10 0 50 100 150
SCALE OF FEET
5 0 10 20 30 40
SCALE OF METRES
PRESBYTERY
QUIRE
NORTH TRANSEPT
TOWER
SOUTH TRANSEPT
SITE OF DORMITORY
NAVE
SITE OF CLOISTER
SITE OF REFECTORY
SERVICE PASSAGE
TOWER
TOWER
OUTER PARLOUR
SITE OF KITCHEN
CELLARER'S RANGE

Gisborough Priory

On 16th May 1289 a plumber descending from the roof of Gisborough Priory church, where he had been soldering cracks in the lead over the south transept, placed on the dry beams his iron pans with their burning coals. His boys came down later without looking to the fire; the roof lead was left to melt and flowed over like lava. Apart from the south aisle wall of the nave and the west front, everything was destroyed—building, ornaments, relics, vestments, books. So perished the middle one in time of three churches on this spot. Its predecessor had been late Norman, and it was replaced by what must have been a masterpiece in Decorated style, to judge from scanty evidence preserved.

The priory stands now within the grounds of Gisborough Hall, though the Lord Gisborough of 1932 appointed as its guardians the Commissioners of Works, since raised to a Ministry. Eighty giant limes in a circle make an impressive curtain on the south, and other attractive neighbours on private property include chestnuts with trunks up to 23 feet in girth, a rose garden, fishpond, and stone octagonal dovecote. But the feature that arrests the gaze of every visitor is the east end of the presbytery, which stands on a pleasant breezy greensward to its original height of 97 feet and is unblemished apart from its lost tracery and the wall beneath the great window, probably broken through intentionally in the Romantic era to create a vista.

This glorious east end, which has been praised equally with work at Ripon and Howden, contains a window 56 feet high and 23 feet wide. Its ornate head springs from clusters of slender shafts with capitals of leaves and acorns. On the jambs are superimposed shields, some bearing the arms of Brus of Skelton, who founded the priory. It has been calculated that the tracery was of seven lights supporting a circle filled with trefoils and flanked by buttresses projecting some ten feet. There is a sharp contrast between the central gable and the horizontal tops to the aisle ends, where again are windows adorned with foliage and pinnacles. An advanced idea for the presbytery was that its triforium and clerestory—the second and third levels—were combined in a single arch. The effect was that they formed with the main arcade a two-storey composition: 'a landmark in the development of northern Gothic'. Externally the buttresses, all with crockets and finials, and their niches with brackets for statues, take the eye.

East end of church, a solitary but nearly perfect fragment

Nothing else is to be seen of the church save some foundations at the towered west end, a few bases of piers in the nave, and a piece of the south transept; but we know the nine bays of the presbytery with the eight of the nave together extended 352 feet. Byland Abbey and Beverley Minster were thus surpassed. West and south of the cloister, excavation has brought to light parts of the cellarer's range, including a vaulted undercroft; these belong to the middle, or thirteenth-century, phase of building.

In Anglo-Norman times there were two gatehouses, each equipped for putting up members of specified families; and one of them, shorn of its lodging, still stands in the north-west corner of the precinct. A variety of round arches and an acutely pointed vault confirm the age of this gracious relic.

Dedicated to the Virgin Mary and granted to Augustinian canons, Gisborough Priory was established by Robert de Brus, forbear of the Scottish Kings but then a Yorkshire baron, with the approval of Pope Calixtus the Second. The antiquary Camden (1551–1623) accepted 1119 as the date, though Walter of Hemingburgh far earlier had preferred 1129. In fact there were two charters. Twenty carucates and two existing plough-lands were thrown in with whole manors to provide an endowment uncommonly rich. Several de Brus lords were buried here, notably he who in Edward the First's reign competed against John Baliol for the Scottish throne. The community was usually prosperous, except for some decades after the fire; and with an annual income given in 1535 as £628 6s. 8d., the fourth biggest in Yorkshire, it easily escaped suppression among the first batch of monasteries. It became a Christmas present to the King in 1539. Land and buildings were leased to Commissioner Legh, passing in 1550 to the Chaloner family.

One canon of this house, William, quit his Order for the Cistercians and became abbot of Fountains. Another who rose to sub-prior here was the chronicler Walter of Hemingburgh. Prior John Whitby in 1505 resigned to go on pilgrimage to the Holy Land and died there. The last prior, Robert Pursglove, was suffragan bishop of Hull when for a healthy pension he signed the deed of surrender to Henry the Eighth.

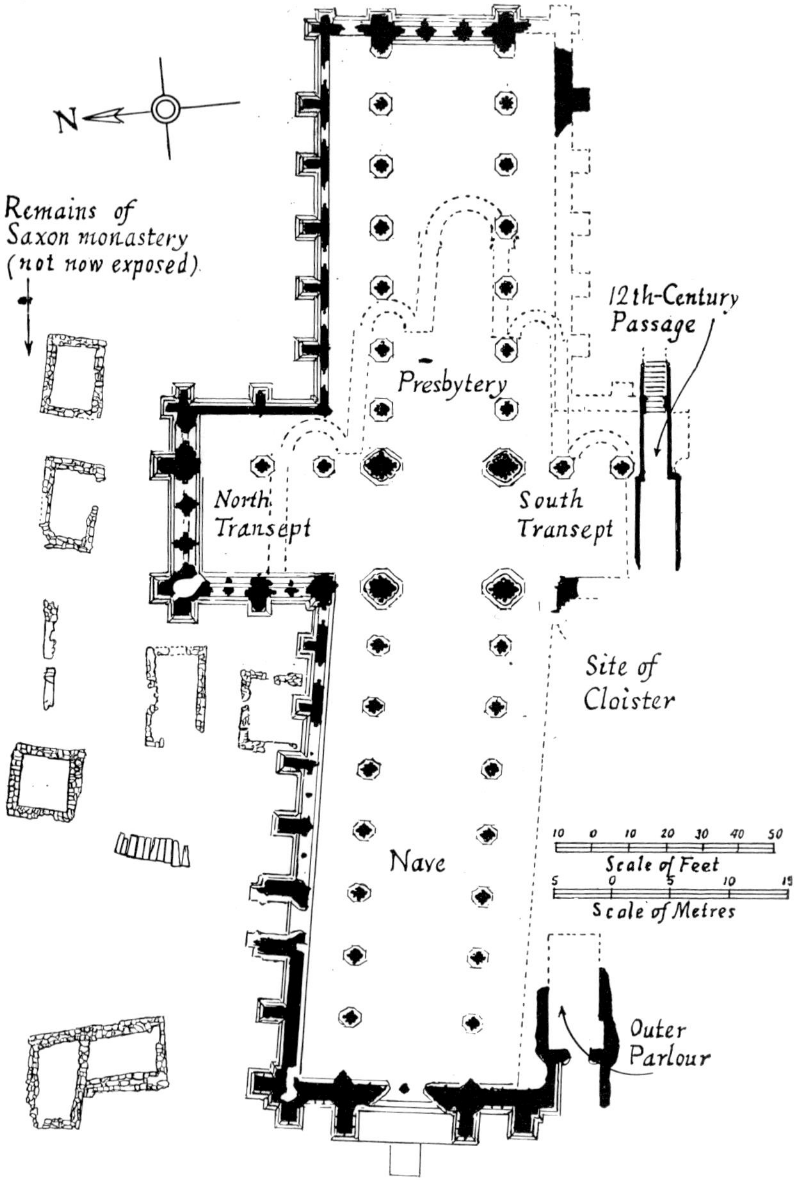

N
Remains of
Saxon monastery
(not now exposed)
12th-Century
Passage
Presbytery
North
Transept
South
Transept
Site of
Cloister
Nave
10 0 10 20 30 40 50
Scale of Feet
5 0 5 10 15
Scale of Metres
Outer
Parlour

Whitby Abbey

Wilfrid's eloquence or Hilda's piety, Oswy's vow or Caedmon's song, even Robin Hood's astounding archery from the tower—whatever we think of first on the east cliff at Whitby will be Anglo-Saxon, for a monastery stood there 1,300 years ago. Accordingly truth and fable are entangled beyond hope of unravelling, but the legends are so delightful that they must be repeated. Scott recognized this when he introduced into *Marmion* the nuns on a voyage from 'high Whitby's cloistered pile'.

Fossil forms and ammonites abounding on the hillside were serpents St. Hilda deprived of their heads and turned to stone. When that holy abbess died, a nun at the daughter house of Hackness heard supernatural tolling and beheld her passing to heaven. In sunlight or in moonlight her shrouded ghost may glimmer among the ruins. So sacred is the spot that birds alighting from a flight over the North Sea drop their pinions in homage (Camden was not too late a scholar to give credence to this; and Henry the Eighth's Commissioners remarked that Hilda was worshipped). Caedmon, an unlettered farm boy of her time, sleeping in a stable, broke into poetry when called on in a dream to sing the beginning of all created things. In 1159 we meet the edifying tale of an aged hermit who, mortally wounded with boar-staves by three sprigs of nobility out hunting, forgave them on penance of holding their lands from the abbot of Whitby and bringing him tribute of stakes every Ascensiontide.

Factually we start with King Oswy of Northumbria, who undertook if victorious at Winwaed against the heathen Penda of Mercia to found a dozen monasteries. In 657 he augmented that pledge by giving his infant daughter into the care of Hilda, who was summoned from Hartlepool to take charge at Whitby of a double house for men and women. Much mentioned in Bede's history, this achieved fame for both devotion and learning. The Northumbrian royal family chose it for their tombs. The

Looking along presbytery towards east end